921
LOV

CPS – MORRILL SCHOOL

Nat Love.

34880030028935

921
LOV

Penn, Sarah.

Nat Love.

34880030028935

$21.25

DATE			

S.G.S.A. FUND
MORRILL SCHOOL

**CPS – MORRILL SCHOOL
CHICAGO PUBLIC SCHOOLS
6011 S ROCKWELL STREET
CHICAGO, IL 60629
04/06/2005**

BAKER & TAYLOR

PRIMARY SOURCES OF
FAMOUS PEOPLE IN AMERICAN HISTORY™

NAT LOVE

AFRICAN AMERICAN COWBOY

SARAH PENN

rosen central
Primary Source™

The Rosen Publishing Group, Inc., New York

To Eric Rothschild

Published in 2004 by The Rosen Publishing Group, Inc.
29 East 21st Street, New York, NY 10010

Copyright © 2004 by The Rosen Publishing Group, Inc.

First Edition

All rights reserved. No part of this book may be reproduced in any form without permission in writing from the publisher, except by a reviewer.

Library of Congress Cataloging-in-Publication Data
Penn, Sarah.
Nat Love: African American cowboy / by Sarah Penn.
  p. cm. — (Primary sources of famous people in American history)
Summary: Surveys the life of Nat Love, African American cowboy, renowned for his riding, roping, and sharpshooting.
Includes bibliographical references (p.) and index.
ISBN 0-8239-4116-7
ISBN 0-8239-4188-4 (pbk.)
6-pack ISBN 0-8239-4315-1
1. Love, Nat, 1854–1921—Juvenile literature. 2. African American cowboys—West (U.S.)—Biography—Juvenile literature. 3. Cowboys—West (U.S.)—Biography—Juvenile literature. 4. West (U.S.)—Biography—Juvenile literature. [1. Love, Nat, 1854–1921. 2. Cowboys. 3. West (U.S.) 4. African Americans—Biography.]
I. Title. II. Series.
F594.L892 P46 2003
978'.00496073'0092—dc21

                                                                              2002155748

Manufactured in the United States of America

Photo credits: cover, p. 5 © Bettmann/Corbis; p. 4 Library of Congress, Washington, D.C./The Bridgeman Art Library; pp. 6, 25 Kansas State Historical Society; pp. 7, 15 (bottom) Library of Congress, Geography and Map Division; pp. 9, 13, 23, 26 © North Wind Picture Archives; p. 11 Western History Collection, University of Oklahoma; p. 12 Library of Congress, Prints and Photographs Division, HABS, ARIZ, 11-POST.V, 3-1; pp. 15 (top, NS-772), 17 (C-34), 18 (X-32050), 20 (X-33925) Denver Public Library, Western History Collection; p. 16 Phillips, Fine Art Auctioneers, New York/ The Bridgeman Art Library; p. 19 Courtesy of the Montana Historical Society, Gift of the Artist; pp. 21, 22, 27, 29 Rare Book, Manuscript, and Special Collections Library, Duke University.

Designer: Thomas Forget; Photo Researcher: Rebecca Anguin-Cohen

CONTENTS

1 A BOY DREAMS TO SEE THE WORLD

Nat Love was born in 1854 in Davidson County, Tennessee. The members of his family were slaves on a tobacco plantation. He had a sister, Sally, and a brother, Jordan. The Civil War ended slavery in 1865. Nat's family was free, but they had no money. Nat's father died. As a young teenager, Nat became the head of the family.

African American slaves worked on American lands for more than 200 years. Their work was unpaid. They often worked from sunrise to sunset.

Slavery ended in America in 1865.
Nat Love left Tennessee for adventure.
He went to the Wild West.

The family planted crops to make money. Meanwhile, pioneers traveled west of the Mississippi River. They went to settle unclaimed land. Many went in search of gold. Nat's goal was to see the world. He imagined the West would be full of excitement and adventure. Nat would not leave his family members until they could support themselves.

After the Civil War (1861–1865), people began to move out West. They were called pioneers. The government gave them land for free.

Some pioneers left from Tennessee. Tennessee was a land of hills and farmland. Nat helped with his family's small farm. He saved money for his dream to go out West.

As a teenager, Nat learned to tame wild horses. He became an excellent rider. One day he won a horse in a raffle. He sold it for $100. Nat gave half of the money to his mother. He used the rest of the money to begin his new life. On February 10, 1869, Nat headed for Dodge City, Kansas.

TRAINING HORSES

To "break" a horse means to tame a wild horse. Taming a wild horse is hard and dangerous work. A horse trusts the cowboy who breaks him. This process makes it easy for them to work together.

This drawing shows cowboys
breaking a wild horse. Nat learned
how to tame horses alone.

2 THE LIFE OF A COWBOY

Nat Love was fifteen years old when he arrived in Dodge City. The town was known for wild saloons and gambling. Many cowboys would spend time there between cattle drives. Nat's excellent horseback-riding skills earned him a job as a cowboy. The Duval Outfit from Texas hired Nat. They taught him to use a gun and a lariat.

DID YOU KNOW?

In the Duval Outfit, Nat was known as Red River Dick.

Dodge City, Kansas, earned a name for being wild.
Cowboys often used the town for drinking and
fighting. Nat found his first adventures in Dodge City.

Cattle drives often took months to take a herd between ranches. Cowboys and cattle would have to battle bad storms with no shelter. Other problems were fights with Indians, bandits, and buffalo stampedes. In 1872, Nat received a better job from the Pete Gallinger Company. He moved to their huge ranch in Gila River, Arizona.

Nat moved to Gila River, Arizona, in search of better work. Nat might have lived in a house like this one made of adobe (mud brick).

Cattle drives often stretched more than a mile. A dozen cowboys or more worked a drive. Nat learned to live in the open air on cattle drives.

3   A CONTEST IN SOUTH DAKOTA

On one cattle drive, Love traveled from Texas to Deadwood, South Dakota. The cowboys delivered almost 3,000 steer there on July 3, 1876. Over the next few days, Love entered a cowboy contest. Each cowboy had to rope, throw, tie, bridle, saddle, and mount a wild mustang horse. Love did it in the least time of only nine minutes. He won $200.

CATTLE DRIVES

Ranches raised cattle or other livestock. They would sell livestock to other ranches. Cattle drives were the earliest way of moving cattle from one ranch to another.

The top photo shows a scene from the Buffalo Bill Wild West Show. It played in towns to show people how cowboys worked. Nat ran cattle drives up to ranches in South Dakota *(map)*.

A shooting contest was held next. Love had learned to shoot a gun well. He entered the contest to try and win more money. Targets were lined up a short distance away. Whoever placed the most shots in the center of the target would win. Love placed fourteen shots in the bull's-eye. This earned him the title "Deadwood Dick."

People in the eastern United States heard about cowboys. The cowboy became a kind of hero. Artists began to show cowboys in their art.

Guns were everyday tools in the Old West. A good shot could put most bullets in a black bull's-eye target. Nat was a very good shot with his gun.

4 TROUBLE WITH THE INDIANS

Later in 1876, Love was alone looking for lost cattle in the prairie. A group of Indians attacked him. They shot him and his horse. When Love awoke, he found himself in an Indian camp. They decided to make him a member of their tribe. The Indians thought they could use a brave, strong man on their side.

Plains Indians lived in small camps. They traveled around often. They followed the buffalo herds for food.

Indians did not often see black men. They thought black men might be white men wearing painted disguises. This scene shows Indians trying to rub off the "paint" of a captured black cowboy.

The Indians healed Love's wounds. He went along with this for a while. Love knew that once the tribe trusted him, he could escape. One night he stayed awake while the Indians were asleep. He quietly stole one of their best horses and escaped. Love returned to the Gallinger Company in Arizona.

Western cities in the late 1800s were a melting pot. People of all ethnic backgrounds lived around each other.

Nat Love could ride any kind of horse. He rode without a saddle when he escaped his Indian captors.

The cowboys were surprised and happy to see Nat Love again. They had given him up for dead. Love began working again.

The cowboys were known to get a bit wild. One night, they were in Fort Dodge. Love and the other cowboys were having a good time. Love decided to rope a cannon and bring it back to camp.

Nat drew a picture of the time he tried to steal a town's cannon. Cowboys liked to play pranks like this. Nat roped the cannon's barrel like he would rope a calf.

Horses are strong animals. Cowboys used their horses for most of their work. A horse was helpful in bringing a cow back to the herd.

Love's idea was to use it to fight the Indians. He roped the cannon and used a horse to pull on it. He quickly found out that the cannon was too heavy to pull. Love was arrested. The sheriff, Bat Masterson, knew these cowboys were not bad guys. He released Nat Love.

DID YOU KNOW?

Bat Masterson was a famous cowboy and buffalo hunter. At 22, Bat became the sheriff of Ford County, Kansas. Fort Dodge is in that county.

Bat Masterson knew all about cowboys. He knew that most were good guys. He often overlooked their pranks.

5 LIFE IN THE WEST CHANGES

Love moved to Denver, Colorado. There he fell in love with a woman named Alice. Nat and Alice married on August 22, 1889.

By 1890, towns and factories began to take over the West. Trains began to move cattle across the country. This was faster, safer, and cheaper than cattle drives. Love retired from life as a cowboy.

Denver, Colorado, was a busy city in 1889. It was once a huge cattle town. By 1890 factories drew people from the farms to work in the city.

Nat Love worked as a cowboy for 20 years. By 1890, Nat had to think more about his family. He left the open range and got a city job.

Love needed a job to support himself and his family. He became a Pullman porter on the Denver and Rio Grande Railroad. Before he died, Love wrote a book about his adventures.

The Life and Adventures of Nat Love was published in 1907. Some people consider many cowboy stories to be "tall tales." He died in 1925.

NAT THE STORYTELLER

Nat's sometimes puffed up the story of his life to make it seem more exciting.

Nat Love wrote the story of his life while he worked as a train porter. He wanted to share his adventures with the public. His book helped tell one story about cowboy life in the American West.

TIMELINE

1854—Nat Love is born into slavery in Davidson County, Tennessee.

1861-1865—The Civil War is fought.

1865-1869—Nat Love and his family are no longer slaves. They make a life of their own.

1869—Nat goes to Dodge City, Kansas. He becomes a cowboy in the Duval Outfit. He moves to Texas, where their ranch is based.

1872—Nat becomes a cowboy in the Pete Gallinger Company. He moves to their large ranch in southern Arizona.

1876—Nat earns the title of "Deadwood Dick."

1877—Nat tries to rope a cannon in Dodge City, Kansas.

1889—Nat marries Alice.

1890—Nat ends his career as a cowboy to become a Pullman porter for the railroads.

1907—*The Life and Adventures of Nat Love* is published.

1925—Nat Love dies.

GLOSSARY

cannon (KAN-uhn) A heavy gun that fires large metal balls.

lariat (LA-ree-uht) A lasso or long rope used to catch animals.

legacy (LEG-uh-see) Something handed down from one generation to another.

pioneer (PYE-uh-NEER) One of the first people to work in a new and unknown area.

plantation (plan-TAY-shun) A large farm found in warm climates where crops such as tobacco, coffee, tea, and cotton are grown.

slavery (SLAYV-ree) When someone is owned by another person and thought of as property.

stampede (stam-PEED) When people or animals make a sudden, wild rush in one direction usually because something has frightened them.

steer (STEER) A young male of the domestic cattle family raised especially for it's beef.

WEB SITES

Due to the changing nature of Internet links, the Rosen Publishing Group, Inc., has developed an online list of Web sites related to the subject of this book. This site is updated regularly. Please use this link to access the list:

http://www.rosenlinks.com/fpah/nlo

PRIMARY SOURCE IMAGE LIST

Page 4: Edwin Austin Abbey engraving titled *Covering the Seed*, appearing in *Harper's Weekly*, April 24, 1875.

Page 6: Illustration titled *Transportation—Covered Wagons* appearing in *Harper's Weekly*, September 1862.

Page 7: 1862 engraved map of Tennessee, by J. T. Lloyd. It is currently housed at the Library of Congress, Washington, DC.

Page 11: Late nineteenth-century photo by John R. Lovett of Dodge City, Kansas. It is currently housed at the University of Oklahoma, Norman, OK.

Page 12: 1938 photograph of farmhouse in Gila River, Arizona, by Frederick A. Eastman. It is currently housed at the Library of Congress, Washington, DC.

Page 15 (top): Photograph of cowboy riding bucking horse for Buffalo Bill's Wild West Show, circa 1901. It is currently housed at the Denver Public Library, Denver, CO.

Page 16: 1889 bronze sculpture titled *The Bronco Buster* by Frederic Remington. It is currently housed in a private collection.

Page 18: Photograph of Native American (Plains) camp, circa 1880. It is currently housed at the Denver Public Library, Denver, CO.

Page 19: Painting titled *Big Medicine* by Charles M. Russell. It is currently housed at the Montana Historical Society, Helena, MT.

Page 20: Hartwell & Hamaker photograph of a scene in Phoenix, Arizona, circa 1899. It is currently housed at the Denver Public Library, Denver, CO.

Page 21: Photograph of an illustration by Nat Love titled *A Case of Breaking the Horse or Breaking My Neck*, appearing in his autobiography, *The Life and Adventures of Nat Love*, 1907. It is currently housed at the University of North Carolina, Chapel Hill, NC.

Page 22: Photograph of an illustration by Nat Love titled *I Rope One of Uncle Sam's Cannon—Fort Dodge, Kan.*, appearing in his autobiography *The Life and Adventures of Nat Love*, 1907. It is currently housed at the University of North Carolina, Chapel Hill, NC.

Page 23: Hand-colored engraving of a Frederic Remington illustration.

Page 26: Illustration of Denver, Colorado, city street, circa 1880.

Page 27: Photograph of Nat Love and family, circa 1907, appearing in his autobiography *The Life and Adventures of Nat Love*. It is currently housed at the University of North Carolina, Chapel Hill, NC.

Page 29 (left): Photograph of the cover illustration by Nat Love to his autobiography *The Life and Adventures of Nat Love*. It is currently housed at the University of North Carolina, Chapel Hill, NC.

Page 29 (right): Photograph of Nat Love titled *The Close of My Railroad Career*, appearing in his autobiography *The Life and Adventures of Nat Love*. It is currently housed at the University of North Carolina, Chapel Hill, NC.

INDEX

ABOUT THE AUTHOR

Sarah Penn writes children's books and designs and makes quilts. She lives with her husband, two children, and four cats in Providence, Rhode Island.